SCRIPTURES & PRAYERS FOR
DELIVERANCE FROM EVIL

50 DAYS OF PRAYER TO OVERCOME DARKNESS AND FIND GOD'S PROTECTION

CYRIL OPOKU

Scriptures & Prayers for Deliverance from Evil: 50 Days of Prayer to Overcome Darkness and Find God's Protection

© 2025 Cyril Opoku. PrayerScripts. All rights reserved.

No part of this publication may be reproduced, stored in a retrieval system, or transmitted in any form or by any means—electronic, mechanical, photocopy, recording, or otherwise—without the prior written permission of the publisher, except in the case of brief quotations used in reviews, articles, or devotionals.

Published by *Quest Publications*

ISBN: 978-1-988439-57-0

Cover design by *Quest Publications (questpublications@outlook.com)*

Unless otherwise indicated, all Scripture quotations are taken from the World English Bible (WEB), which is in the public domain. For more information, visit: www.worldenglish.bible

This book is a work of devotional encouragement. It is not intended to replace biblical study, pastoral counsel, or professional therapy.

Printed in the United States of America.

First Edition: July 2016
Second Edition: June 2025

For more books like this, visit *PrayerScripts:* https://prayerscripts.org

Contents

Preface v
How to Use This Devotional vi
Day 1: When Time Runs Out, God Remains 1
Day 2: Besieged but Not Broken 2
Day 3: Awakened to Freedom 3
Day 4: Escaped the Snare 4
Day 5: Divine Rescue 5
Day 6: Flee the Captive Chains 6
Day 7: Turning Back the Wicked 7
Day 8: Shield Me From Their Schemes 8
Day 9: Eyes Fixed on Deliverance 9
Day 10: Exposing the Hidden Plot 10
Day 11: Guard Me From the Violent 12
Day 12: Silent Arrows, Sudden Fall 14
Day 13: Traps Set for the Foolish 15
Day 14: God Above the Chaos 16
Day 15: Fear Not the Enemy's Roar 18
Day 16: Unshaken in the Battle 19
Day 17: Break Their Plans, O God 20
Day 18: A Window of Escape 22
Day 19: When the Enemy Withdraws 23
Day 20: Fear Not the Siege 24
Day 21: Justice in Your Hands 26
Day 22: Lifted from the Deep 27
Day 23: Held in God's Timing 28
Day 24: Untouched by the Stones 29
Day 25: Escape from Their Hands 30

Day 26:	Lowered to Freedom	31
Day 27:	Carried by the Spirit	32
Day 28:	Escaped Like a Bird	33
Day 29:	Eyes on the Rescuer	34
Day 30:	Guard Me From Their Snares	35
Day 31:	Pull Me from the Net	36
Day 32:	Strength in Brokenness	37
Day 33:	Chains Broken, Doors Opened	38
Day 34:	My Refuge in the Roar	40
Day 35:	Plots Known, Still in Control	42
Day 36:	Silent Judgment	43
Day 37:	Confidence That Holds	44
Day 38:	Rescued from the Lion's Mouth	45
Day 39:	Strength When Alone	46
Day 40:	Faith Over Fear	47
Day 41:	Lions Silenced	48
Day 42:	Faith That Conquers	49
Day 43:	Spirit Empowered	50
Day 44:	Stand Firm, Resist Strong	51
Day 45:	Deliverance Near	52
Day 46:	Shelter from the Roar	53
Day 47:	Sweetness from the Strong	54
Day 48:	Preserved from All Evil	55
Day 49:	Faithful Protection from the Evil One	56
Day 50:	Deliver Us from Evil	57

Epilogue *58*
Encourage Others with Your Story *59*
More from PrayerScripts *60*

Preface

Evil is real. It creeps in through fear, lies, temptation, injustice, and despair. It shows up in spiritual attacks, unexpected betrayals, heavy oppression, and unseen forces working to unravel the peace God has promised. We weren't meant to face this darkness in our own strength. We were meant to fight from a place of faith—armed with the Word of God and anchored in prayer.

This book was born out of that conviction.

Scriptures & Prayers for Deliverance from Evil is not just a devotional—it is a spiritual companion for anyone walking through hard places, facing hidden battles, or seeking shelter from the storm. Over these 50 days, you will pray the Scriptures that speak directly to God's power to deliver, defend, and protect. Each prayer is deeply rooted in a specific Bible verse—written to help you connect personally with God, cry out for His help, and find peace in His promises.

These are not lofty, distant prayers. They are honest, heartfelt, and often written from the valleys where many of us have stood. They echo the cries of David, the courage of Daniel, the faith of the early church, and the victory of Christ Himself. Whether you are praying for yourself or standing in the gap for someone else, may each day lead you deeper into God's presence and remind you: evil does not get the final word—God does.

May the Spirit guide you, the Word strengthen you, and the love of Christ sustain you as you walk through these pages and declare truth over your life. Deliverance is not just a hope—it is a promise for those who belong to Him.

In His Strength,
Cyril O. (June 2025)

How to Use This Devotional

This 50-day devotional is designed to be both personal and flexible—something you can lean on in quiet moments, desperate prayers, or daily time with God. Here's how you can make the most of it:

1. **Set Aside Sacred Time**
   Choose a time each day—morning, evening, or during a lunch break—when you can pause, reflect, and invite God into your space. Even ten focused minutes can create room for His peace.

2. **Start with the Scripture**
   Each day begins with a key Scripture that anchors the theme. Read it slowly. Read it aloud. Let it speak to your soul before you move on. You may want to journal or underline words that stand out.

3. **Pray the Prayer Personally**
   The prayer that follows is written in the first person—so you can pray it as your own. Speak it aloud or silently from your heart. Let the words give voice to what you may struggle to say on your own.

4. **Linger with God**
   After the prayer, pause. Breathe. Listen. Let the Spirit bring peace, conviction, healing, or comfort. Some days may feel emotional—others may feel calm. Trust that God meets you either way.

5. **Return When Needed**
   These prayers aren't just for a one-time journey. Revisit them when life gets heavy again. Mark the ones that resonate most. Share them with someone who needs strength.

This devotional is not about perfect discipline—it's about consistent grace. Whether you journey through all 50 days in a row or return whenever evil rises, may these Scriptures and prayers be a light in your darkness, a comfort in your distress, and a steady reminder that **God is with you, for you, and working through it all.**

You're not alone. Let's walk this journey together—one prayer at a time.

Day 1: When Time Runs Out, God Remains

> For man also doesn't know his time. As the fish that are taken in an evil net, and as the birds that are caught in the snare, even so are the sons of men snared in an evil time, when it falls suddenly on them.
> —Ecclesiastes 9:12 WEB

Lord, I come before You with a heart that knows how uncertain this life is. Just as Your Word says in Ecclesiastes, I do not know my time. Like fish caught in an evil net or birds taken in a snare, I see how suddenly trouble can fall—how evil can spring upon a person without warning. I confess, Father, that this truth humbles me. I cannot control the day of my testing, and I cannot outrun the snare when it appears.

But I do not walk in fear, because I trust in You. You are the One who sees the hidden traps. You are the Deliverer who can break every net and free every captive. Even when evil rises like a sudden storm, You remain my refuge. You remain my shield. I take shelter in You, not because I am strong, but because You are.

So I surrender today, Lord—my plans, my timing, my need to be in control. I surrender the fear of what I cannot see. I place my trust in Your wisdom, knowing that You number my days and order my steps. Though I may not know the time or the season when danger comes, I know the One who holds time in His hands.

Deliver me from every hidden evil. Rescue me from every unseen snare. Keep me close to You, anchored in Your truth, walking in Your light, guarded by Your mercy. I rest in the promise that nothing surprises You, and nothing can overcome me when I dwell in You.

In Jesus' name, Amen.

Day 2: Besieged but Not Broken

> They also who seek after my life lay snares. Those who seek my hurt speak mischievous things, and meditate deceits all day long.
> —Psalms 38:12 WEB

Father, I feel the weight of opposition around me. Just as Your Word says in Psalm 38, there are those who lay traps for my downfall, who speak deceit and imagine mischief day and night. Sometimes, Lord, it feels overwhelming—like the very air is thick with schemes and the intentions of others are not for my good. But in the midst of it all, I look to You.

You are my defender when I cannot defend myself. You are the One who sees every hidden plot and every whispered lie. You know the pain of betrayal and the sting of false words. So I bring my wounded heart to You, and I lay down my fear, my frustration, my need to make it right on my own.

I trust You to be my shield. I trust You to deliver me from evil that I cannot see and from plans formed in secret places. You are my stronghold, my hiding place, my peace in the middle of this battle. Though others may plot harm, You work all things together for my good. Though I am surrounded, I am not abandoned. Though the enemy whispers, You speak truth over me.

So I rest in You, God of justice. Deliver me, not only from their snares but from the bitterness that could take root in me. Keep my spirit pure and my heart set on You. I will wait on You, and I will not be moved, because You are faithful.

In Jesus' name, Amen.

Day 3: Awakened to Freedom

> ...and they may recover themselves out of the devil's snare, having been taken captive by him to his will.
> —2 Timothy 2:26 WEB

Lord, I lift my heart to You in humility and hope. Your Word speaks of those who are taken captive by the enemy, trapped in his snare and doing his will without even knowing it. And I know, Father, that without Your mercy, I too could fall into that place. So today, I come with surrender, asking You to deliver me fully from every deception, every trap, every lie that would keep me bound.

Thank You that in Your grace, You offer recovery—You offer repentance that opens my eyes and softens my heart. I don't want to live blind to Your truth or enslaved by the enemy's schemes. I want to walk in freedom, alert and awake, doing Your will—not his.

So I yield to You now. Break every chain that's tried to hold me. Open my eyes to see clearly. Restore my heart to obedience and trust. I choose Your will over mine, Your wisdom over the world's, Your truth over every false voice. Even where I've wandered, You are able to restore me.

Thank You for being the God who rescues, who delivers from evil, and who gives me the power to stand in Your light. Keep me close to You, Lord, walking in truth and not falling back into the traps that once held me.

In Jesus' name, Amen.

Day 4: Escaped the Snare

> Our soul has escaped like a bird out of the fowler's snare. The snare is broken, and we have escaped.
> —Psalms 124:7 WEB

Ever-Present Savior, I lift my voice to You with gratitude—because my soul has escaped like a bird from the snare of the fowler's trap. You are the One who broke every chain and shattered every trap set against me.

Deliver me again, Lord, from every hidden danger that threatens to ensnare me. Rescue me when I am vulnerable, guard me when I am unaware, and lead me safely through every trial. Let no weapon or scheme of the enemy prevail over me.

Your Word says, "Our soul is escaped as a bird out of the snare of the fowlers: the snare is broken, and we are escaped." And I know this is my story—this is my testimony. You broke the trap the enemy set for me. You shattered the cords that tried to hold me. What once had a grip on my soul, no longer has power, because You intervened.

There were moments I didn't even know how close I was to being caught—how near the danger truly was. But You knew. You saw it all, and in Your mercy, You made a way of escape. You didn't leave me in the hands of the enemy. You didn't let the snare tighten around me. You delivered me, and I am free.

Keep me near to You, Lord. Teach me to walk wisely, to live watchfully, and to trust continually in Your power to deliver. No matter what lies ahead, I know the snare is broken—and I am free.

In Jesus' name, Amen.

Day 5: Divine Rescue

> For he will deliver you from the snare of the fowler, and from the deadly pestilence.
> —Psalms 91:3 WEB

Mighty Protector, I come to You asking for deliverance from every snare the enemy has laid for me. Rescue me from the traps I cannot see and the hidden dangers that seek to harm my soul. Shield me, Lord, from every pestilence and evil that threatens my life.

Let Your faithful hand be upon me, guarding me day and night. Surround me with Your protection so that no weapon formed against me shall prosper. Strengthen my heart to trust in Your power and keep me safe in Your refuge.

There have been times when fear tried to grip me—when the noise of trouble and the whisper of lies tried to cloud my faith. But You, Lord, are faithful. You draw me close under the shelter of Your wings. You rescue me from what I could never escape on my own. You lift me out of harm's way and cover me with Your love.

I trust in Your protection—not just from what I see, but from every hidden threat, every secret plan, every snare meant to entangle my soul. You are the God who delivers—not once, but again and again. My heart is steady because You are near.

Thank You, Father, for being my shield. Thank You for breaking the power of fear and rescuing me from evil. I will not be shaken, because I dwell in the shadow of the Almighty.

In Jesus' name, Amen.

Day 6: Flee the Captive Chains

> Free yourself, like a gazelle from the hand of the hunter, like a bird from the snare of the fowler.
> —Proverbs 6:5 WEB

Lord, I come to You urgently, knowing there are times when I have been caught—by words spoken too quickly, by choices made in haste, by traps I didn't see until it was almost too late. Your Word tells me to deliver myself like a roe from the hand of the hunter, and like a bird from the hand of the fowler. And so I come running to You, my Deliverer, crying out for Your help and strength.

Give me the wisdom and courage to flee from every entanglement that threatens my freedom in You. Teach me to be quick to repent, quick to obey, and quick to run from compromise. Let me not linger in places of danger or delay when You call me to rise and escape.

I know that I cannot free myself without You—but I also know that by Your Spirit, You empower me to rise and break free. So I surrender my pride, my stubbornness, and my comfort, and I choose freedom over fear. I choose obedience over delay. I choose life over the trap.

Thank You for always making a way of escape. Thank You for loving me enough to warn me, to guide me, and to pull me back when I drift. I run to You now, Lord—into Your arms, into Your wisdom, into Your deliverance.

In Jesus' name, Amen.

Day 7: Turning Back the Wicked

> Let a cry be heard from their houses, when you bring a troop suddenly on them; for they have dug a pit to take me, and hidden snares for my feet.
> —Jeremiah 18:22 WEB

Lord, You see what I cannot. You hear what is whispered in secret. Your Word in Jeremiah reveals the cries of those whose enemies seek their downfall, who dig pits for their feet and devise harm with no cause. And though evil may rise around me, I take comfort in knowing that nothing escapes Your justice.

I bring my pain and fear to You, O Righteous Judge. When others seek to ensnare me, when words are used like weapons and plans are made to harm, I will not repay evil with evil. I will not be moved by vengeance. Instead, I place it all in Your hands—every injustice, every false word, every pit dug beneath my path.

Deliver me from the evil intentions of others. Surround me with Your favor as with a shield. Let not their plans succeed, for I belong to You. Teach me to walk in integrity even when surrounded by trouble. Strengthen me not to fear, but to trust that You, Lord, are my Defender and Avenger.

I release the burden of retaliation. I choose peace over bitterness, trusting that You will uphold what is right and true. Be my guard, my justice, my deliverer from every hidden evil.

In Jesus' name, Amen.

Day 8: Shield Me From Their Schemes

> Keep me from the snare which they have laid for me, from the traps of the workers of iniquity. Let the wicked fall together into their own nets, while I pass by.
> —Psalms 141:9-10 WEB

Lord, I lift my eyes to You, my constant protector and guide. Just as Your servant David prayed, so do I: "Keep me from the snares which they have laid for me, and the gins of the workers of iniquity." I know that evil schemes are real—plots crafted in darkness, meant to trap the feet of the innocent. But I trust You to guard my steps.

Keep me, Lord, from falling into what the enemy has prepared. Let not the traps set by the wicked catch me unaware. Be my shield in hidden places. Be my light when the path is unclear. I look to You to preserve me—not only from harm, but from responding in fear, anger, or revenge.

And as Your Word says, let the wicked fall into their own nets, while I escape unharmed. I don't desire their destruction, Lord—I desire Your justice. I desire Your peace. I ask You to turn the plans of the enemy back upon themselves and to preserve my soul in righteousness.

Lead me safely through the danger. Keep my heart pure and my eyes fixed on You. I know You are faithful to deliver, and I rest in the safety of Your hands.

In Jesus' name, Amen.

Day 9: Eyes Fixed on Deliverance

> My eyes are ever on Yahweh, for he will pluck my feet out of the net.
> —Psalms 25:15 WEB

Lord, my eyes are ever toward You. I fix my gaze on You because I know You alone can pluck my feet out of the net. So many times I've found myself tangled—stuck in confusion, caught in fear, or snared by the consequences of my own choices. But even then, You never turn away.

You are the God who rescues. You see the nets before I do, and even when I step into them, You do not leave me there. With gentleness and power, You reach down and lift me out. You break the cords that bind and steady me once again on solid ground.

So I choose to keep looking up. Not at the traps. Not at the fear. But at You—my Deliverer, my Redeemer, my constant help. I trust You to lead me, to guide me away from what entangles, and to walk with me into freedom.

Thank You for being so faithful. Thank You for seeing me, rescuing me, and never letting the net define my story. I belong to You, and I will keep my eyes on You always.

In Jesus' name, Amen.

Day 10: Exposing the Hidden Plot

> For among my people are found wicked men. They watch, as fowlers lie in wait. They set a trap. They catch men. As a cage is full of birds, so are their houses full of deceit. Therefore they have become great, and grew rich. They have grown fat. They shine; yes, they excel in deeds of wickedness. They don't plead the cause, the cause of the fatherless, that they may prosper; and they don't judge the right of the needy. "Shouldn't I punish for these things?" says Yahweh. "Shouldn't my soul be avenged on such a nation as this?
> —Jeremiah 5:26-29 WEB

Lord, You see what lies hidden in the hearts of men. Your Word in Jeremiah declares that among the people are those who lay wait, like hunters setting traps, who set snares to catch others and grow rich through deceit. They cage the innocent like birds, their houses filled with stolen gain, and they grow great, fat, and powerful—yet they do not plead the cause of the orphan or defend the needy.

My heart grieves, Lord, at the injustice that still lives in our world. The wicked prosper while the righteous suffer. Evil advances while the helpless are forgotten. But I know that You are a God of justice, and You will not turn a blind eye forever.

Search my heart, O God. Let there be no trace of such wickedness in me. Deliver me from every deceptive way—whether it traps others or entraps my own soul. Guard me from the seduction of gain without mercy, power without compassion, success without righteousness.

I cry out for deliverance—not only for myself, but for the oppressed, the silenced, the ones caught in nets they did not weave. Rise up, O Lord, and let justice roll down like waters. Let mercy and truth prevail in my life and in my land. Make me one who pleads the cause of the poor, who stands for what is right, who reflects Your heart.

You are the God who sees, the God who delivers, and the God who will repay all according to their deeds. I take refuge in Your righteousness, and I long for Your kingdom to come.

In Jesus' name, Amen.

Day 11: Guard Me From the Violent

> He lies in wait near the villages. From ambushes, he murders the innocent. His eyes are secretly set against the helpless. He lurks in secret as a lion in his ambush. He lies in wait to catch the helpless. He catches the helpless, when he draws him in his net. The helpless are crushed. They collapse. They fall under his strength. He says in his heart, "God has forgotten. He hides his face. He will never see it." Arise, Yahweh! God, lift up your hand! Don't forget the helpless.
> —Psalms 10:8-12 WEB

Lord, I see the cruelty and injustice in this world, just as Your Word describes. The wicked lie in wait in secret places, ambushing the innocent. They murder the helpless and watch their prey like a lion in hiding, ready to pounce on the poor and draw them into their nets. They crush others with their strength and say in their hearts, "God has forgotten… He hides His face… He will never see it."

But I know the truth, Lord. You are not blind. You are not silent. You are not distant. You see every hidden trap. You hear every cry of the afflicted. You feel the weight of injustice even more than we do. So I lift my voice with David and say, "Arise, O Lord." Stand against those who oppress. Break the arm of the wicked. Expose their schemes. Defend the helpless and rescue those caught in their cruelty.

And God, when I feel overwhelmed by what I see—when evil seems to win and justice seems delayed—help me remember who You are. You are the God of the oppressed, the Defender of the fatherless, the Judge of all the earth. You do not forget. You do not forsake. You will act in Your perfect time.

Strengthen me to stand for what is right, even when darkness surrounds. Keep my heart soft, my eyes fixed on You, and my trust anchored in Your justice and love.

In Jesus' name, Amen.

Day 12: Silent Arrows, Sudden Fall

> They encourage themselves in evil plans. They talk about laying snares secretly. They say, "Who will see them?" They plot injustice, saying, "We have made a perfect plan!" Surely man's mind and heart are cunning. But God will shoot at them. They will be suddenly struck down with an arrow.
> —Psalms 64:5-7 WEB

Lord, I come to You knowing that there are those who secretly lay traps and sharpen their tongues like swords, planning injustice in the dark. As Your Word says, they encourage one another in evil, saying, "Who shall see them?" They carefully hide their snares, thinking no one will uncover their schemes.

But You, O God, are not unaware. You see what is done in secret. You know every hidden word, every buried motive, every plan meant to harm. And You promise that You Yourself will shoot at them with a sudden arrow—that their own tongues will bring them down. You are the God who defends the innocent and exposes the schemes of the wicked.

So I take comfort in Your justice. I do not have to fight in my own strength, nor carry the burden of proving every wrong. You are my Defender. You are my Advocate. You will answer deceit with truth, and cruelty with Your holy justice.

Deliver me from every snare, seen and unseen. Keep my heart clean, and my trust rooted in You. Let all who look on see Your hand at work, and let my life be a testimony of Your faithfulness to those who take refuge in You.

In Jesus' name, Amen.

Day 13: Traps Set for the Foolish

> for their feet run to evil. They hurry to shed blood. For in vain is the net spread in the sight of any bird: but these lay wait for their own blood. They lurk secretly for their own lives.
> —Proverbs 1:16-18 WEB

Lord, Your Word warns me that the feet of the wicked run to evil, and they make haste to shed innocent blood. Their path is filled with violence and their hearts devise destruction, but they do not realize—they are setting a trap for their own lives. They lay in wait for others, but it is their own souls that will be caught.

God, keep me far from such a path. Let me never be drawn into the way of the violent, the proud, or the deceitful. Guard my heart from the temptation to retaliate, to scheme, or to seek gain at another's loss. Help me to walk in wisdom, in peace, and in righteousness. Let my steps follow the way of life, not destruction.

Deliver me, Lord, from every alliance that leads toward harm. Open my eyes to the hidden dangers of sin that may look like shortcuts or strength but end in ruin. I want no part in what offends You. I want my life to reflect Your justice, Your mercy, and Your truth.

Thank You that You warn me through Your Word. Thank You for showing me the end of the wicked so I might choose the path of the upright. Keep my soul from every snare, and my heart fully Yours.

In Jesus' name, Amen.

Day 14: God Above the Chaos

> You who have purer eyes than to see evil, and who cannot look on perversity, why do you tolerate those who deal treacherously, and keep silent when the wicked swallows up the man who is more righteous than he, and make men like the fish of the sea, like the creeping things, that have no ruler over them? He takes up all of them with the hook. He catches them in his net, and gathers them in his dragnet. Therefore he rejoices and is glad.
> —Habakkuk 1:13-15 WEB

Lord, You are of purer eyes than to behold evil, and You cannot look on iniquity with approval. Yet sometimes, I confess, I struggle to understand why the wicked seem to triumph—why those who deal treacherously go unpunished, why the righteous suffer while the deceitful prosper. Like Habakkuk, I see the nets of the wicked cast wide, drawing in the helpless like fish, and my heart aches.

But even in my questioning, I turn to You. You are still holy. You are still just. You see every trap, every injustice, every cry that rises from the oppressed. You are not blind to evil, and You are not absent in the storm. Though the wicked rejoice in their gain and worship the tools of their cruelty, You will not let their injustice stand forever.

So I bring You my confusion and lay it at Your feet. I bring You my sorrow and trust it into Your hands. I know You are working, even when I don't understand. I know You will deliver, even when the net seems to tighten.

Strengthen my heart, Lord. Help me wait on Your justice without growing bitter or fearful. Let me rest in the truth of who You are—a

God of mercy, power, and perfect righteousness. You will deliver. You will judge rightly. And until that day, I will keep trusting You.

In Jesus' name, Amen.

Day 15: FEAR NOT THE ENEMY'S ROAR

> For I have heard the defaming of many, "Terror on every side! Denounce, and we will denounce him!" say all my familiar friends, those who watch for my fall. "Perhaps he will be persuaded, and we will prevail against him, and we will take our revenge on him." But Yahweh is with me as an awesome mighty one. Therefore my persecutors will stumble, and they won't prevail. They will be utterly disappointed, because they have not dealt wisely, even with an everlasting dishonor which will never be forgotten.
> —Jeremiah 20:10-11 WEB

Lord, there are times when fear surrounds me—when whispers of betrayal echo louder than truth, and the pressure to give up feels strong. Just as Jeremiah cried, I too have felt the sting of mockery, the weight of being misunderstood, and the fear of plots laid in secret. "Terror on every side," they say—waiting for me to stumble, hoping for my fall.

But in the midst of it all, I declare with confidence: You, O Lord, are with me as a mighty and terrible one. You are my strength and my defender. Those who rise against me may be many, but they will not prevail, for You stand beside me with power and justice in Your hands.

You search the heart. You know my thoughts and motives. You see the truth when others twist it. I will not be overcome, because You are greater than every voice of fear and every scheme of the enemy.

So I take courage in Your presence. I find peace in knowing that You fight for me. Let not my heart grow weary, and let not my soul be silenced. You are my deliverer from evil, and I place my full trust in You. In Jesus' name, Amen.

Day 16: Unshaken in the Battle

> All day long they twist my words. All their thoughts are against me for evil. They conspire and lurk, watching my steps, they are eager to take my life. Shall they escape by iniquity? In anger cast down the peoples, God.
> —Psalms 56:5-7 WEB

Lord, You see the wounds that words can leave. All day long, they twist my words, stir up strife, and plot to harm me. Their thoughts are bent on evil, their attacks relentless. They gather in secret, watching my steps, waiting for the moment to strike, as if my very life were theirs to take.

But I will not be shaken, because You are my refuge. I bring this pain to You—the injustice, the fear, the weight of being misunderstood and pursued without cause. You are the righteous Judge, and I trust You to deal with those who rise against me. You will not let their violence go unanswered, nor their cruelty unpunished.

Though I am surrounded, I am not alone. Though they war against me, You fight for me. You see every tear, every step, every word. I rest in Your justice and find peace in Your presence.

Deliver me, O God, from their schemes. Break the power of their words, and silence every lie. Let truth rise, and let Your name be glorified in my life as You deliver me from evil.

In Jesus' name, Amen.

Day 17: Break Their Plans, O God

> Yahweh, keep me from the hands of the wicked. Preserve me from the violent men who have determined to trip my feet. The proud have hidden a snare for me, they have spread the cords of a net by the path. They have set traps for me. Selah. I said to Yahweh, "You are my God." Listen to the cry of my petitions, Yahweh. Yahweh, don't grant the desires of the wicked. Don't let their evil plans succeed, or they will become proud. Selah. As for the head of those who surround me, let the mischief of their own lips cover them. Let burning coals fall on them. Let them be thrown into the fire, into miry pits, from where they never rise.
> —Psalms 140: 4-6, 8-10 WEB

Lord, I cry out to You—my shield, my strength, my deliverer. Keep me, O Lord, from the hands of the wicked. Preserve me from those who seek to destroy, who stir up violence and set traps along my path. Their hearts are full of pride, their tongues like sharpened blades, but I take refuge in You.

You are the God of my salvation. You hear the cries of the afflicted. You do not turn away from those who call on You in truth. So I lift my voice to You now—rescue me from the evil that hunts me, from those who plot behind closed doors and speak harm with hidden tongues.

Let not their desires prevail, Lord. Do not allow their schemes to prosper. As they lift themselves up in pride and pour out poison with their words, let their plans turn back on them. Let burning coals fall upon them; let them be cast into the fire, into deep pits from which they cannot rise.

You are the defender of the righteous. You uphold the cause of the innocent. I trust You to protect me, to fight for me, and to deliver me from every evil work.

In Jesus' name, Amen.

Day 18: A Window of Escape

> Saul sought to pin David to the wall with the spear; but he slipped away out of Saul's presence, and he stuck the spear into the wall. David fled, and escaped that night. Saul sent messengers to David's house, to watch him, and to kill him in the morning. Michal, David's wife, told him, saying, "If you don't save your life tonight, tomorrow you will be killed." So Michal let David down through the window. He went away, fled, and escaped.
> —1 Samuel 19:10-12 WEB

Lord, I thank You that even when danger surrounds me—when the enemy rises up with violence and throws weapons meant to destroy—You are still in control. Just as Saul hurled the spear at David, trying to take his life, You made a way of escape. You provided a window in the dark. You stirred someone's heart to help. You protected when the threat was real and the moment was urgent.

I hold onto that truth today. When I feel targeted, misunderstood, or hunted by forces I can't fully explain, I remember that You are my deliverer. You make a way when there seems to be no way. You open windows of grace when doors are shut. You raise up allies when I feel alone.

Thank You for watching over me in the night hours. Thank You for sending help at just the right time. Even in crisis, You are my refuge. I don't rely on my own strength or strategy—I rely on You. Hide me in Your mercy. Lead me in Your wisdom. Deliver me from the hand of every enemy, and let my life be a testimony to Your faithful protection. In Jesus' name, Amen.

Day 19: WHEN THE ENEMY WITHDRAWS

> Saul went on this side of the mountain, and David and his men on that side of the mountain; and David hurried to get away for fear of Saul; for Saul and his men surrounded David and his men to take them. But a messenger came to Saul, saying, "Hurry and come; for the Philistines have made a raid on the land!" So Saul returned from pursuing David, and went against the Philistines. Therefore they called that place Sela Hammahlekoth.
> —1 Samuel 23:26-28 WEB

Lord, I see how close the enemy can come—how the danger can press in from every side, like Saul surrounding David, ready to seize him. There are moments in my life where I feel hemmed in, trapped by fear, by opposition, by burdens too heavy to carry. It feels like the enemy is just a step away from victory.

But just as You did for David, You intervene. You are never late. You are never unaware. When the trap is nearly closed, You send a messenger. You shift the battle. You turn the enemy away. You are the God who delivers at the last moment, the God who rescues when escape seems impossible.

So I will not fear, even when the pressure builds, even when the path grows narrow. I trust You to be my rescue. I trust You to move on my behalf, to send help from heaven, to scatter those who rise against me. What the enemy meant for harm, You will use for my deliverance.

Thank You for being my Defender in every tight place. Thank You for knowing exactly when and how to act. You are faithful, and I rest in the shadow of Your mighty hand.

In Jesus' name, Amen.

Day 20: Fear Not the Siege

> Now in the fourteenth year of king Hezekiah, Sennacherib king of Assyria came up against all the fortified cities of Judah, and took them. Isaiah said to them, "Tell your master this: 'Yahweh says, "Don't be afraid of the words that you have heard, with which the servants of the king of Assyria have blasphemed me. Behold, I will put a spirit in him, and he will hear news, and will return to his own land. I will cause him to fall by the sword in his own land."'"
> —2 Kings 18:13; 19:6-7 WEB

Lord, there are times when the enemy seems overwhelming—when, like Sennacherib of Assyria, evil rises with force, surrounding what is precious, threatening what You have promised. Just as he came against Judah and laid siege to fortified cities, so do the forces of fear, destruction, and intimidation rise up in my life, seeking to steal, kill, and destroy.

But You, O Lord, are not shaken by earthly power. You spoke through Your servant and said, "Be not afraid of the words… which the servants of the king of Assyria have blasphemed Me." You promised to send a spirit upon the enemy, to cause confusion in their camp, to drive them back by Your hand—not mine.

So I stand on that promise now. I will not fear the threats or the noise of the enemy. I will not bow to the pressure or the fear that tries to break in. You are the God who defends His people. You are the One who fights for me. You will turn back the enemy in ways I cannot imagine, and his plans will fall by his own sword.

Thank You, Lord, for the power of Your Word. Thank You for the assurance of Your presence. Though evil may rise, You rise higher.

Though the enemy roars, You speak peace. I trust in Your deliverance—not just from trouble, but from the fear of it. In Jesus' name, Amen.

Day 21: Justice in Your Hands

> He frustrates the plans of the crafty, So that their hands can't perform their enterprise. He takes the wise in their own craftiness; the counsel of the cunning is carried headlong. They meet with darkness in the day time, and grope at noonday as in the night. But he saves from the sword of their mouth, even the needy from the hand of the mighty. So the poor has hope, and injustice shuts her mouth.
> —Job 5:12-16 WEB

Lord, I praise You because You are the One who frustrates the devices of the crafty, so that their hands cannot perform their plans. You take the wisdom of the wise in their own craftiness, and the counsel of the cunning is brought to nothing. Even when the enemy schemes in secret, You see it all. You overturn their plans and protect the innocent.

When I feel powerless against deception, when it seems like injustice is winning and evil has the upper hand, I remember that You are my Defender. You break the traps of the oppressor. You shine light into darkness. You save the poor from the sword and from the mouth of the mighty. You do not forget the cry of the afflicted.

Thank You for standing on behalf of the humble. Thank You for being the God who sees, who hears, and who acts with justice and mercy. Let the plans of the wicked come to nothing, Lord, and let the voice of the righteous be lifted up. Let those who are crushed rise with hope, and let injustice be silenced by the power of Your truth.

You are my rescue. You are my strength. I trust in Your faithful hand to deliver me from all evil. In Jesus' name, Amen.

Day 22: Lifted from the Deep

> He sent from on high. He took me. He drew me out of many waters. He delivered me from my strong enemy, from those who hated me; for they were too mighty for me.
> —Psalms 18:16-17 WEB

Lord, I thank You with all my heart—for when I was drowning in sorrow, when the waters of trouble overwhelmed me and I was sinking beneath the weight of it all, You reached down from on high and took hold of me. You didn't let me go. You drew me out of many waters.

You rescued me from my strong enemy, from those who were too powerful for me. When I was too weak to stand, You became my strength. When I couldn't find a way out, You became my deliverance. You saw me in my distress and came to my aid—not because I was worthy, but because You are merciful.

Thank You, Lord, for saving me when I couldn't save myself. Thank You for pulling me from the depths and lifting me up in Your arms of grace. You are my Deliverer, my Rock, my ever-present help in trouble. I will trust You through every storm, knowing You are always near to rescue.

In Jesus' name, Amen.

Day 23: Held in God's Timing

> They sought therefore to take him; but no one laid a hand on him, because his hour had not yet come.
> —John 7:30 WEB

Lord, I rest in the truth of Your sovereign hand. Just as it was written of Jesus, though they sought to take Him, no man laid a hand on Him because His hour was not yet come. You are the God of perfect timing. Nothing touches me outside of Your will. No enemy can prevail against me unless You allow it, and even then, it serves Your greater purpose.

When fear rises, when threats feel near, I remind my soul that I am held by You. My days are in Your hands. You have appointed my times and my seasons. You are never late, and You are never caught off guard.

So I refuse to live in fear of what man can do. I will not be anxious about tomorrow or consumed by the pressures of today. You are my shield, and unless You permit it, no hand can touch me, no plan can succeed. You protected Your Son until His hour had come—and in the same way, You will fulfill Your purpose in my life.

Thank You for being my covering, my protector, and the Author of my story. I surrender to Your timing, and I rest in Your power.

In Jesus' name, Amen.

Day 24: Untouched by the Stones

> Therefore they took up stones to throw at him, but Jesus was hidden, and went out of the temple, having gone through the middle of them, and so passed by.
> —John 8:59 WEB

Lord, I stand in awe of Your wisdom and power. When the crowd picked up stones to cast at Jesus, He slipped away—untouched, unharmed—because His time had not yet come. You, Father, made a way of escape when death was at the door. You shielded Him until His mission was complete.

And I trust You to do the same for me. When I am surrounded by danger or threatened by voices that do not understand me, I remember that I am hidden in You. You know how to guard me. You know how to lead me through the crowd and out of the trap. What the enemy means for harm, You turn for good.

Let me walk in confidence, not fear—in obedience, not retreat. I will not fear stones thrown in anger or judgment spoken in haste, for You are my hiding place. You will protect me until my purpose is fulfilled. And when the moment is right, You will bring me through, just as You brought Your Son through every moment ordained by heaven.

Thank You, Lord, for divine covering, for sovereign timing, and for faithful deliverance.

In Jesus' name, Amen.

Day 25: Escape from Their Hands

> They sought again to seize him, and he went out of their hand.
> —John 10:39 WEB

Heavenly Father, I marvel at the peace and power You displayed in the life of Jesus. Though they sought again to take Him, He escaped out of their hand. You were His refuge, His shield, His ever-present help—and I know You are the same for me.

There are moments when I feel surrounded—by pressure, by threats, by spiritual battles I cannot see. But I remember that just as Jesus walked away untouched, so too can I walk in the safety of Your presence. The enemy may try again and again, but he has no power over me outside of Your will. I am not in his hands—I am in Yours.

So I trust You, Father. I trust Your timing, Your wisdom, and Your power to deliver. You are my escape when I feel trapped, my hiding place when I feel exposed. Let me walk with the same confidence Jesus had, knowing that You go before me and stand behind me. No weapon formed against me shall prosper, for I am held by the hand of Almighty God.

Thank You for Your faithfulness. Thank You for Your covering. Thank You that even when the enemy comes close, You are closer still.

In Jesus' name, Amen.

Day 26: Lowered to Freedom

> In Damascus the governor under King Aretas guarded the Damascenes' city, desiring to arrest me. Through a window I was let down in a basket by the wall, and escaped his hands.
> —2 Corinthians 11:32-33 WEB

Lord, I thank You that even when I am surrounded, You make a way. Just as Paul was pursued in Damascus—watched at the gates by those who sought to take his life—you provided an unexpected escape. Through a window in the wall, in a basket lowered by faithful hands, You delivered him from the enemy's grip.

You are the same faithful God today. When opposition rises, when I feel trapped with no clear path forward, I will not despair. You are the God of hidden windows and quiet rescues. You make a way through walls. You use what seems small—like a basket and a rope—to do something mighty.

Help me trust You when I can't see the way out. Help me believe that even in my weakness, You are strong, and even in closed places, You are working. Send the right people at the right time. Open the right window. Lower me into Your perfect will, even if it's not how I imagined.

Thank You for Your protection, Your provision, and Your faithfulness. I will rest in the truth that no plot against me can prevail when You are the One writing my story.

In Jesus' name, Amen.

Day 27: CARRIED BY THE SPIRIT

> When they came up out of the water, the Spirit of the Lord caught Philip away, and the eunuch didn't see him any more, for he went on his way rejoicing. But Philip was found at Azotus. Passing through, he preached the Good News to all the cities, until he came to Caesarea.
> —Acts 8:39-40 WEB

Lord, I stand in awe of Your power and Your mysterious ways. Just as You caught Philip away after he had fulfilled Your assignment, and the eunuch went on his way rejoicing, I see how You move with purpose—how You place Your servants exactly where they need to be, and then carry them forward in Your perfect timing.

You are the God who lifts, who sends, who redirects without delay. You waste nothing and overlook no one. Philip disappeared from one place and reappeared in another, yet in all of it, Your Spirit was leading. So I surrender to that same Spirit today. Use me where You will. Move me when it's time. Let me be faithful in every moment, and when the mission is done, carry me onward into the next.

And just like the eunuch, may I always go on my way rejoicing—knowing that every encounter, every divine appointment, every change of direction is in Your hands. You are the God of both departure and arrival, and I trust You to lead me step by step.

Thank You for divine timing, divine movement, and divine joy.

In Jesus' name, Amen.

Day 28: Escaped Like a Bird

> Blessed be Yahweh, who has not given us as a prey to their teeth. Our soul has escaped like a bird out of the fowler's snare. The snare is broken, and we have escaped. Our help is in Yahweh's name, who made heaven and earth.
> —Psalms 124:6-8 WEB

Blessed be You, Lord, who have not given me as prey to the enemy's teeth. When I look back on the snares set before me, on the moments where evil closed in and danger felt near, I see now—it was You who kept me. You who stepped in. You who broke the grip of destruction.

My soul has escaped like a bird out of the snare of the fowlers. The snare is broken, and I am escaped! Not by my strength, not by my wisdom, but by Your mercy and power. You shattered what was meant to bind me. You destroyed what was meant to end me. You have delivered me, and I lift my voice in praise.

My help is in the name of the Lord, who made heaven and earth. The One who holds the universe holds me. And because of that, I will not fear. I will not be moved. You are my Deliverer, my Sustainer, and my Song.

In Jesus' name, Amen.

Day 29: Eyes on the Rescuer

> My eyes are ever on Yahweh, for he will pluck my feet out of the net.
> —Psalms 25:15 WEB

Lord, my eyes are ever toward You. In a world full of distractions, dangers, and hidden traps, I fix my gaze on You alone—for You are the One who will pluck my feet out of the net. I confess, there are moments when I've wandered close to snares laid by the enemy, times when I've stepped into things I didn't see coming. But You, in Your mercy, have never taken Your eyes off me.

You are the God who rescues. You reach down into the tangled places and lift me out. You break the cords that hold me, and You set my feet on solid ground. I look to You because I trust You. I look to You because You've never failed me. And even when I can't see the full path ahead, I know You're guiding every step.

Keep my eyes upward, Lord—not on the danger, not on the noise, but on You. Be my vision, my guard, and my guide. Thank You for being the One who delivers me time and time again.

In Jesus' name, Amen.

Day 30: Guard Me From Their Snares

> Yahweh, keep me from the hands of the wicked. Preserve me from the violent men who have determined to trip my feet. The proud have hidden a snare for me, they have spread the cords of a net by the path. They have set traps for me. Selah.
> —Psalms 140:4-5 WEB

Lord, I come to You as my refuge and my defender. Keep me, O Lord, from the hands of the wicked. Preserve me from the violent, from those who plot to push me off the path You've laid before me. Their hearts are set on destruction, their minds on deceit. But my trust is not in my own strength—it is in You.

They have hidden snares for me in secret places, spread nets by the wayside, and laid traps to catch me unaware. But You, O God, are not unaware. You see what is hidden. You know what is spoken in darkness. You walk before me, and You watch over me.

I ask You now to guard my steps, to uncover every trap, and to deliver me from every scheme of the enemy. Let not the plans of the wicked succeed, and let not their violence overtake me. Be my shield in battle, my wisdom in confusion, and my safety in every storm.

In Jesus' name, Amen.

Day 31: Pull Me from the Net

> Pluck me out of the net that they have laid secretly for me, for you are my stronghold.
> —Psalms 31:4 WEB

Lord, into Your hands I commit my way, for You are my strength and my stronghold. Pull me out of the net that they have secretly laid for me—for You are my refuge. You see what I cannot see. You know every hidden trap, every whispered lie, every scheme woven in the dark.

When I feel surrounded, when the path seems unclear, I remember that You are the God who delivers. You do not leave me to wander into danger alone. You go before me. You fight for me. You shield me beneath the shadow of Your wings.

So I take refuge in You. I trust that You will pull me out—not just from the snares of others, but from the doubts, fears, and temptations that try to entangle my soul. You are faithful. You are near. You are mighty to save.

Thank You, Lord, for being my constant deliverer and my place of safety.

In Jesus' name, Amen.

Day 32: STRENGTH IN BROKENNESS

> The Philistines laid hold on him, and put out his eyes; and they brought him down to Gaza, and bound him with fetters of brass; and he ground at the mill in the prison. However the hair of his head began to grow again after he was shaved. Samson called to Yahweh, and said, "Lord Yahweh, remember me, please, and strengthen me, please, only this once, God, that I may be at once avenged of the Philistines for my two eyes."
> —Judges 16: 21-22, 28 WEB

Lord, there are moments when I feel like Samson—bound by consequences, weakened by failure, and led by forces I once had strength to resist. Just as the Philistines took him, gouged out his eyes, and made him grind in the prison house, I too have felt the weight of shame and regret. Yet, even in that place of brokenness, Your mercy was not finished.

Your Word says that Samson's hair began to grow again. And I hold onto that hope—because with You, even after failure, restoration begins. You are the God of second chances, the One who remembers us when we call upon You in humility and truth.

So like Samson, I cry out: "O Lord God, remember me, I pray thee, and strengthen me, I pray thee, only this once." Not for my glory, but for Yours. Let Your strength rise again in me. Let Your Spirit move through me, even now. Restore what was lost. Redeem what was broken. Use my life, even the painful parts, for Your victory.

You are the God who brings power out of weakness, and purpose out of pain. I trust You to work through me again.

In Jesus' name, Amen.

Day 33: CHAINS BROKEN, DOORS OPENED

> Peter therefore was kept in the prison, but constant prayer was made by the assembly to God for him. The same night when Herod was about to bring him out, Peter was sleeping between two soldiers, bound with two chains. Guards in front of the door kept the prison. And behold, an angel of the Lord stood by him, and a light shone in the cell. He struck Peter on the side, and woke him up, saying, "Stand up quickly!" His chains fell off from his hands. When they were past the first and the second guard, they came to the iron gate that leads into the city, which opened to them by itself. They went out, and went down one street, and immediately the angel departed from him. When Peter had come to himself, he said, "Now I truly know that the Lord has sent out his angel and delivered me out of the hand of Herod, and from everything the Jewish people were expecting." When Herod had sought for him, and didn't find him, he examined the guards, and commanded that they should be put to death. He went down from Judea to Caesarea, and stayed there. On an appointed day, Herod dressed himself in royal clothing, sat on the throne, and gave a speech to them. The people shouted, "The voice of a god, and not of a man!" Immediately an angel of the Lord struck him, because he didn't give God the glory, and he was eaten by worms and died.
> —Acts 12: 5-7,10-11, 19, 21-23 WEB

Lord, You are the God who sees, the God who hears, and the God who delivers. When Herod stretched out his hand to persecute the church, when James was killed and Peter was chained between soldiers, guarded with heavy watch and sealed behind iron gates, You were not silent. You sent an angel. You lit up the darkness. You broke the chains, opened the doors, and led Peter out to freedom.

Even when it seemed impossible—even when all hope looked buried behind bars—You were already moving. You are the God who brings sudden deliverance, who makes a way in the night, and who leads Your people beyond the reach of the enemy.

And when pride rose in Herod's heart, when he took glory for himself and did not give glory to You, You did not overlook it. You struck him down, and all saw that You alone are God. You alone deserve honor, power, and praise.

So I come to You now with deep trust. If I am bound, You can break the chains. If I am surrounded, You can open the gate. If I am afraid, You will send Your peace. And if any rise in pride or cruelty, I know You will deal with them in Your perfect justice.

Thank You for being my Deliverer, my Defender, and my Righteous Judge. I will follow You, even through the gates of iron.

In Jesus' name, Amen.

Day 34: My Refuge in the Roar

For the Chief Musician. To the tune of "Silent Dove in Distant Lands." A poem by David, when the Philistines seized him in Gath. Be merciful to me, God, for man wants to swallow me up. All day long, he attacks and oppresses me. My enemies want to swallow me up all day long, for they are many who fight proudly against me. All day long they twist my words. All their thoughts are against me for evil. They conspire and lurk, watching my steps, they are eager to take my life. Shall they escape by iniquity? In anger cast down the peoples, God. You count my wanderings. You put my tears into your container. Aren't they in your book? Then my enemies shall turn back in the day that I call. I know this, that God is for me. For you have delivered my soul from death, and prevented my feet from falling, that I may walk before God in the light of the living.
—Psalms 56: 1-2, 5-9, 13 WEB

Be merciful unto me, O God. The battle feels relentless. My enemies would swallow me up; they fight against me daily, pressing hard without rest. Their words twist like knives, their thoughts are set against me for evil. All day they wrestle, they conspire, they watch my steps, hoping to bring me down.

But in the midst of their attacks, I turn to You. When I am afraid, I will trust in You. You see my tears. You number them. Not one falls to the ground unnoticed. You have recorded my pain, my wanderings, my cries—they are written in Your book. You are not distant from my sorrow, and You will not ignore the injustice.

This I know: God is for me.

My enemies will turn back when I cry unto You. That alone gives me peace. I walk in the light of Your presence, not in the shadow of their threats. You have delivered my soul from death. Will You not also keep my feet from falling, that I may walk before You in the land of the living?

Thank You, Lord, for Your mercy, for Your nearness, and for the victory You promise. I will trust in You and not be afraid.

In Jesus' name, Amen.

Day 35: Plots Known, Still in Control

> Then the chief priests, the scribes, and the elders of the people were gathered together in the court of the high priest, who was called Caiaphas. They took counsel together that they might take Jesus by deceit, and kill him.
> —Matthew 26:3-4 WEB

Lord, even as the chief priests and elders plotted in secret to take Jesus by subtlety and kill Him, You were still in control. Though evil conspired behind closed doors, though the plan was cloaked in darkness, nothing escaped Your sight. Every scheme, every whisper, every hidden motive was known to You.

And so I take comfort, Lord. When I feel surrounded by opposition, when I sense that there are plans against me I cannot see or understand, I remember this truth: You are never surprised. You are never overpowered. Even when the enemy plots in silence, You are already working for my good.

You allowed the plot against Jesus not because evil triumphed, but because love did. His life was not taken—it was given, according to Your will. And because of that, I trust You with my life. I trust You when I don't see the full picture. I trust You even when it feels like darkness is gathering.

Deliver me from the schemes of the enemy. Hide me under the shadow of Your wings. Give me discernment, courage, and peace as I rest in the safety of Your sovereignty.

In Jesus' name, Amen.

Day 36: Silent Judgment

> But these, as unreasoning creatures, born natural animals to be taken and destroyed, speaking evil in matters about which they are ignorant, will in their destroying surely be destroyed,
> —2 Peter 2:12 WEB

Lord, Your Word speaks of those who speak evil of things they do not understand—like brute beasts, following their own corrupt instincts, destined for destruction. It grieves me to see how truth is twisted, how righteousness is mocked, and how many walk boldly in darkness, unaware of the judgment to come.

But I will not fear their voices. I will not be shaken by their insults. Instead, I lift my eyes to You, the Righteous Judge. You see all. You know all. And You will repay every word, every deed, every rebellion according to truth and justice.

Keep my heart from pride, Lord. Let me not respond to evil with evil or ignorance with anger. Teach me to walk in humility and holiness, with eyes fixed on You. Guard my lips from speaking what I do not understand, and keep me close to Your Word, where wisdom dwells.

Thank You that You are not slow to act, nor blind to corruption. You will judge rightly. Until then, I rest in Your justice, walk in Your truth, and trust in Your power to deliver me from evil.

In Jesus' name, Amen.

Day 37: Confidence That Holds

> for Yahweh will be your confidence, and will keep your foot from being taken.
> —Proverbs 3:26 WEB

Lord, You are my confidence. In a world full of uncertainty, shifting ground, and unseen dangers, I anchor my heart in You. Your Word says that You shall be my confidence and shall keep my foot from being taken—and I believe it with all my soul.

When fear tries to whisper, when the path ahead looks unsure, I choose to trust in You. You see what I cannot. You guard every step I take. You hold me steady when traps are laid before me. You are not just watching over me—you are keeping me, shielding me, guiding me.

I will not lean on my own understanding. I will not put my trust in fleeting strength or human wisdom. I place my confidence in You, the One who never fails, never sleeps, never turns away. Let Your peace rule in my heart, and let Your presence go before me.

Thank You for keeping my foot from being taken, for surrounding me with Your protection, and for being the sure foundation beneath me every day.

In Jesus' name, Amen.

Day 38: Rescued from the Lion's Mouth

> Yahweh says: "As the shepherd rescues out of the mouth of the lion two legs, or a piece of an ear, so shall the children of Israel be rescued who sit in Samaria on the corner of a couch, and on the silken cushions of a bed."
> —Amos 3:12 WEB

Lord, Your Word in Amos speaks of the shepherd rescuing from the mouth of the lion just two legs or a piece of an ear. It's a sobering image—one of devastation, yet also of a remnant, a rescue, a sign that even in judgment, You still preserve what is Yours.

There are times I've felt torn by life's battles—like I've lost too much, like only fragments remain. But even then, You are still my Deliverer. Even when the enemy has done great harm, You are able to pull something out of the wreckage. You redeem what is broken. You recover what others would leave behind.

So I bring You the torn pieces, the remnants of hope, the bruised and battered places of my heart. I trust that You are the Shepherd who sees, who reaches in, who rescues—even when it's almost too late. You are not finished with me. What remains is enough for You to rebuild, restore, and redeem.

Thank You for holding on to what others would throw away. Thank You for being the God of the remnant, the God who delivers even when all seems lost.

In Jesus' name, Amen.

Day 39: STRENGTH WHEN ALONE

> But the Lord stood by me, and strengthened me, that through me the message might be fully proclaimed, and that all the Gentiles might hear; and I was delivered out of the mouth of the lion. And the Lord will deliver me from every evil work, and will preserve me for his heavenly Kingdom; to whom be the glory forever and ever. Amen.
> —2 Timothy 4:17-18 WEB

Mighty Deliverer, You stood with me and strengthened me when no one else did. When I felt abandoned, when I stood alone in the face of resistance, You were there—closer than breath, stronger than fear. You gave me courage. You gave me words. You gave me the power to endure, so that through me, the message could still go forth.

Thank You for rescuing me from the lion's mouth—from danger I could not overcome on my own. Time and again, You have proven Yourself faithful. And I hold onto this promise: that You will deliver me from every evil work and preserve me unto Your heavenly kingdom.

King of glory, finish the work You've started in me. Keep me faithful, keep me steadfast, and keep me walking in Your strength until the very end. To You be glory forever and ever.

In Jesus' name, Amen.

Day 40: Faith Over Fear

> David said to Saul, "Your servant was keeping his father's sheep; and when a lion or a bear came, and took a lamb out of the flock, I went out after him, and struck him, and rescued it out of his mouth. When he arose against me, I caught him by his beard, and struck him, and killed him. Your servant struck both the lion and the bear. This uncircumcised Philistine shall be as one of them, since he has defied the armies of the living God." David said, "Yahweh who delivered me out of the paw of the lion, and out of the paw of the bear, he will deliver me out of the hand of this Philistine." Saul said to David, "Go! Yahweh will be with you."
> —1 Samuel 17:34-37 WEB

Faithful God, the One who has watched over me since my youth, I remember how You were with David when he faced the lion and the bear. Alone in the field, no one saw—but You did. And You gave him strength to strike down the wild beasts that threatened the flock. He didn't boast in himself; he trusted in You.

I cling to that same confidence now. Just as You delivered him from the paw of the lion and the bear, I believe You will deliver me from every challenge that rises before me. No giant, no threat, no enemy can stand against the power of the living God.

Shepherd of my soul, train my hands for battle, but keep my heart soft and full of faith. Let every past deliverance become a testimony that fuels my trust today. You were faithful then; You are faithful now.

In the name of the Lord of hosts, the God of the armies of Israel, I stand and I will not fear.

In Jesus' name, Amen.

Day 41: Lions Silenced

> My God has sent his angel, and has shut the lions' mouths, and they have not hurt me; because as before him innocence was found in me; and also before you, O king, I have done no harm." He delivers and rescues. He works signs and wonders in heaven and in earth, who has delivered Daniel from the power of the lions."
> —Daniel 6: 22, 27 WEB

O God Most High, You are the One who shuts the mouths of lions. Just as You sent Your angel to stand with Daniel in the den, You surround me with Your presence in the darkest places. You see the accusations, the plots, the fear—and yet You allow no harm to touch those who trust in You.

Because Daniel was found innocent before You, You delivered him. And because of the righteousness of Christ in me, I know You hear my cry and cover me with Your hand. You are the living God, steadfast forever. Your kingdom shall never be destroyed, and Your dominion endures through all generations.

You deliver and rescue. You work signs and wonders in heaven and on earth. You shut down every enemy and raise up the humble. I praise You for every unseen battle You've won on my behalf—for every lion You've silenced, every trap You've turned back, and every fear You've conquered.

Keep me walking in integrity. Keep me trusting when the night is long. I know You are near, and You will deliver.

In Jesus' name, Amen.

Day 42: Faith That Conquers

> ...who, through faith subdued kingdoms, worked out righteousness, obtained promises, stopped the mouths of lions,
> —Hebrews 11:33 WEB

Righteous King, You are the rewarder of those who live by faith. Through faith, Your people have conquered kingdoms, worked righteousness, obtained promises, and stopped the mouths of lions. This is not ancient history—it is the living testimony of what You still do today.

You are the same yesterday, today, and forever. And so I believe. I trust not in what I see, but in who You are. I cling to Your Word when the battle rages. I walk forward, even when the outcome is unseen, because I know You honor faith—not strength, not perfection, but a heart that believes You are able.

Strengthen my faith today, Mighty One. Let me walk in the footsteps of those who believed before me. Help me to stand firm, to do what is right, and to hold on until the promise is fulfilled. If lions rise, silence them. If kingdoms oppose, overcome them. If weariness creeps in, refresh me with Your Spirit.

You are the God who delivers through faith. And I am Yours.

In Jesus' name, Amen.

Day 43: Spirit Empowered

> Then Samson went down to Timnah with his father and his mother, and came to the vineyards of Timnah; and behold, a young lion roared at him. Yahweh's Spirit came mightily on him, and he tore him as he would have torn a young goat; and he had nothing in his hand, but he didn't tell his father or his mother what he had done.
> —Judges 14:5-6 WEB

Almighty God, the Spirit of the Lord rushed upon Samson, and in that moment of danger, You filled him with supernatural strength. Though a young lion roared against him, it was no match for the power of Your Spirit. He had no weapon in his hand, yet by Your power, he overcame.

Holy One, I may not face a lion in the flesh, but I do face enemies, temptations, and trials that roar fiercely in my path. On my own, I am not enough. But with Your Spirit resting on me, there is no threat too great, no battle too strong. What I cannot do in my own strength, You accomplish through me by Your power.

So come upon me afresh, O Spirit of the living God. Fill me with boldness, with courage, with divine strength. When fear rises up like a lion, let Your power rise stronger. Let me tear down every obstacle—not by might, nor by power, but by Your Spirit.

You are the God who empowers the weak and gives victory to the surrendered. I depend on You fully.

In Jesus' name, Amen.

Day 44: STAND FIRM, RESIST STRONG

> Be sober and self-controlled. Be watchful. Your adversary, the devil, walks around like a roaring lion, seeking whom he may devour. Withstand him steadfast in your faith, knowing that your brothers who are in the world are undergoing the same sufferings.
> —1 Peter 5:8-9 WEB

Gracious Father, You have warned me to be sober, to be vigilant—for my adversary, the devil, prowls like a roaring lion, seeking whom he may devour. But I will not be overcome, because You have not left me defenseless. You have given me faith, and through faith I will resist him—steadfast, grounded, and firm in the truth.

I know I am not alone in this battle. My brothers and sisters around the world face the same suffering, and yet You are faithful to all who endure. So I stand alert—not in fear, but in readiness. I fix my eyes on You, not the roar. I plant my feet in the victory of Christ, not the shifting threats of the enemy.

Strengthen me, Mighty Defender. Help me to remain rooted in Your Word, clothed in Your armor, watchful in spirit, and unwavering in my trust. And when the enemy presses in, remind me that he is already defeated, and that I belong to the God who always causes me to triumph.

In Jesus' name, Amen.

Day 45: Deliverance Near

> But don't be far off, Yahweh. You are my help: hurry to help me. Deliver my soul from the sword, my precious life from the power of the dog. Save me from the lion's mouth! Yes, from the horns of the wild oxen, you have answered me.
> —Psalms 22:19-21 WEB

O my Strength, be not far from me. Trouble is near, and there is none to help. I feel surrounded—by fear, by sorrow, by voices that threaten to undo me. Yet I lift my cry to You, the God who hears, the God who rescues.

Deliver my soul from the sword, my precious life from the power of the enemy. Save me from the lion's mouth—from every force that seeks to tear me down. You have heard me from the horns of the wild oxen before, and I know You will hear me again.

You are my Defender, my Rescuer, my ever-present help in trouble. Draw near to me now. Strengthen my heart. Rescue me swiftly and completely. Let those who seek my soul see that I am not alone, for the Holy One of Israel stands with me.

I will praise You, even as I wait for deliverance. For You are faithful.

In Jesus' name, Amen.

Day 46: SHELTER FROM THE ROAR

> *A meditation by David, which he sang to Yahweh, concerning the words of Cush, the Benjamite.* Yahweh, my God, I take refuge in you. Save me from all those who pursue me, and deliver me, lest they tear apart my soul like a lion, ripping it in pieces, while there is no one to deliver.
> —Psalms 7:1-2 WEB

O Lord my God, in You do I put my trust. I run to You as my refuge, my shelter, my defender. Save me from those who pursue me—from every voice, every force, every enemy that seeks to tear my soul like a lion, rending it in pieces when there is no one else to deliver.

I do not stand by my own strength. I do not hide behind my own wisdom. I take refuge in You alone. You are the God who sees the hidden dangers and rescues the helpless. When I feel hunted, when the weight of fear presses in, I remember that You are near, mighty to save, and quick to hear the cry of Your child.

So I entrust myself to You again today. Break the grip of every threat. Silence the roar of every lie. Pull me from the teeth of those who seek to harm, and let me rest in the safety of Your steadfast love.

In Jesus' name, Amen.

Day 47: Sweetness from the Strong

> He said to them, "Out of the eater came out food. Out of the strong came out sweetness." They couldn't in three days declare the riddle.
> —Judges 14:14 WEB

Wise and Sovereign God, You are the author of mysteries and the revealer of truth. Just as Samson spoke his riddle—"Out of the eater came forth meat, and out of the strong came forth sweetness"—so often, You bring life from what once brought fear, and blessing from the very places of battle.

I may not always understand what You are doing, but I trust that hidden within my trials are treasures. What once tried to consume me can become the very place You nourish me. What was meant for harm, You turn into sweetness. From the lion's carcass came honey—so from the ruins of my struggle, You bring joy, healing, and unexpected grace.

Help me not to curse the hard places but to wait on You with expectation. Unravel the riddles of my life, Lord. Let me see Your goodness in the things I feared. Let what was once strong against me now feed my soul with testimony.

You are the God of wonders, turning fear into provision and sorrow into praise.

In Jesus' name, Amen.

Day 48: Preserved from All Evil

> Yahweh will keep you from all evil. He will keep your soul. Yahweh will keep your going out and your coming in, from this time forward, and forever more.
> —Psalms 121:7-8 WEB

Faithful Keeper of my life, I hold fast to Your promise: You shall preserve me from all evil—not some, not just the visible—but all evil. You shall preserve my soul. In a world full of hidden dangers and unseen battles, this truth brings peace to my heart. You are not just watching over my path—You are guarding my very soul, the deepest part of who I am.

You preserve my going out and my coming in. In every step, every decision, every place I walk—You are there. From this time forth, and even forevermore, Your protection does not end. It is not limited by time or place. You are the same yesterday, today, and forever.

So I surrender my movements to You—my journeys, my returns, my rising, and my rest. Preserve me from evil that waits in ambush. Shield me from harm that I cannot see. Let no arrow strike, no trap succeed, no darkness consume. Because You, O Lord, are my Keeper.

Preserve me, Lord—from evil thoughts that war against my peace, from dark forces that seek to devour, from subtle lies that twist truth. Surround me with Your presence. Keep my soul steadfast in Your love.

Thank You for surrounding me with a covering that cannot be broken, and for guarding me now and forevermore.

In Jesus' name, Amen.

Day 49: Faithful Protection from the Evil One

> and that we may be delivered from unreasonable and evil men; for not all have faith. But the Lord is faithful, who will establish you, and guard you from the evil one.
> —2 Thessalonians 3:2-3 WEB

My Faithful Protector, I lift my eyes to You—the One who stands with me when the wicked rise and faith seems rare. Your Word says that not all have faith, and I see it, Lord. There are those who oppose truth, who scheme without conscience, who try to shake what You have planted in me. But I will not be afraid, because You are faithful.

You will stablish me. You will strengthen me. You will guard me from the evil one. No matter how loud the threats, how real the pressure, or how subtle the deception—You are the One who keeps me secure. I am not standing on shifting ground. I am held by the God who cannot fail.

Preserve me from spiritual harm. Deliver me from evil people and evil powers. Fortify my heart to remain steady when the world around me trembles. Root me deeper in Your truth, and let nothing pull me away from Your presence.

Thank You that Your faithfulness is not limited by mine. You are my constant covering, my sure defense, and my unshakable hope.

In Jesus' name, Amen.

Day 50: Deliver Us from Evil

> Bring us not into temptation, but deliver us from the evil one. For yours is the Kingdom, the power, and the glory forever. Amen.'
> —Matthew 6:13 WEB

Our Father, Holy and Sovereign, I come to You with the prayer Your Son taught—simple, powerful, and full of trust. Lead me not into temptation, Lord, for I know how easily my heart can be drawn away. Guard my steps from paths that look harmless but lead to ruin. Keep me sensitive to Your voice and strong in the face of weakness.

And deliver me from evil—from every scheme of the enemy, from the subtle lies, from the shadows that try to darken my soul. Rescue me from both the evil around me and the evil that tries to rise within. You alone have the power to break every chain, to silence every accusation, and to make a way of escape when the pressure is too much.

Yours is the kingdom. Yours is the power. Yours is the glory. Not just for today, but forever. So I rest in the truth that You reign, that You fight for me, and that no evil will ever have the final say.

In Jesus' name, Amen.

Epilogue

As you close this book, remember that deliverance is not a one-time event but a lifelong journey. The battle against evil continues, but so does the power and presence of the God who saves. The Scriptures you've prayed over these 50 days are more than words—they are living promises, eternal truths that stand firm when everything else feels uncertain.

Carry these prayers in your heart. Return to them whenever you face new challenges, doubts, or fears. Let them be your shield and your sword, your refuge and your strength. Know that God's protection surrounds you every moment, even when you cannot see it.

You are not alone. The God who delivered David from lions, who shut the mouths of lions for Daniel, who raised Jesus from the grave, is with you now. His light breaks through the darkest night. His love overcomes every shadow. His power is made perfect in your weakness.

Walk forward in confidence, knowing that you are guarded, loved, and deeply held by the Almighty. The enemy may roar, but the King of kings reigns. Your deliverance is sure.

May peace, hope, and victory go with you always.

In Jesus' name, Amen.

Encourage Others with Your Story

If this book has encouraged or strengthened you in your journey toward deliverance, I would be grateful if you could share your experience by leaving a review on Amazon. Your honest feedback not only helps me grow but also encourages others seeking God's protection and peace to find hope through these prayers and Scriptures.

Thank you for letting this book be part of your walk with God. May His deliverance continue to surround you every day!

More from PrayerScripts

SCRIPTURES & PRAYERS FOR DELIVERANCE FROM TROUBLE: 40 DAYS OF PRAYER FOR WHEN LIFE FEELS OVERWHELMING

Are you walking through a season where life feels heavy, hope feels distant, and your prayers feel weak?

Scriptures & Prayers for Deliverance from Trouble is a 40-day journey of honest prayers and powerful Scriptures to help you find peace, strength, and healing when life is overwhelming. Each day offers a personal, Scripture-based prayer written in the language of real faith and raw trust. This devotional isn't about perfect words—it's about real connection with God when you need Him most.

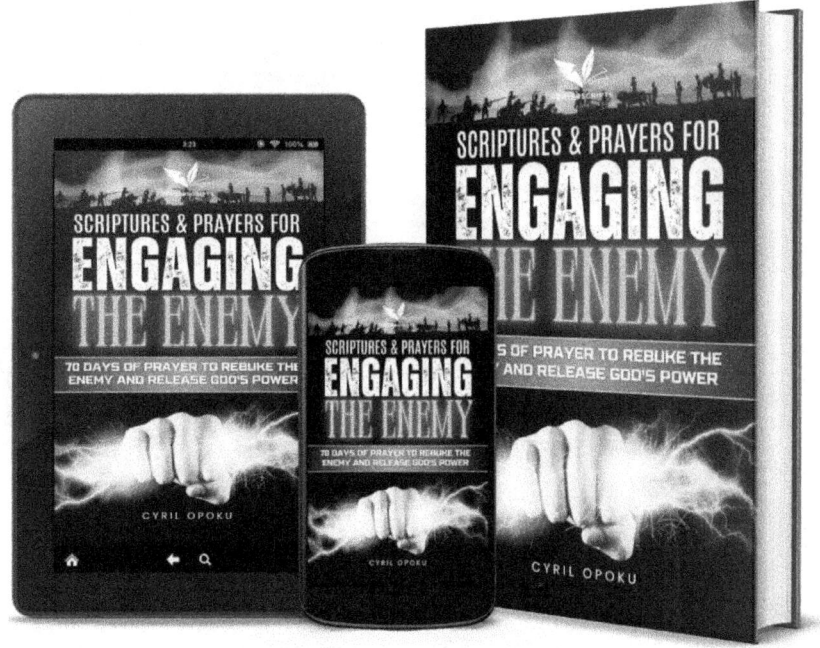

SCRIPTURES & PRAYERS FOR ENGAGING THE ENEMY:
70 DAYS OF PRAYER TO REBUKE THE ENEMY AND RELEASE GOD'S POWER

*You weren't called to run from the battle—
you were anointed to win it.*

Scriptures & Prayers for Engaging the Enemy: 70 Days of Prayer to Rebuke the Enemy and Release God's Power is a bold devotional for believers who are ready to rise, resist, and reclaim what the enemy has tried to steal. If you're tired of feeling spiritually outnumbered, this book will equip you to fight back—with Scripture in your mouth and power in your prayers. Over 70 days, you'll be guided through five strategic phases of spiritual warfare: (1) **Rebuking the Enemy,** (2) **Releasing Terror Upon the Enemy** (3) **Praying for the Fall of the Enemy** (4) **Treading Upon the Enemy** (5) **When Heaven Strikes.**

The war is real. But so is your victory.

SCRIPTURES & PRAYERS FOR COMBATING SPIRITUAL WICKEDNESS:
50 DAYS OF PRAYER TO OVERTHROW WICKED PLANS AND STAND IN GOD'S VICTORY

Are you facing opposition that feels deeper than the natural? Do you sense hidden resistance working against your progress, peace, or purpose? You're not imagining it—and you're not powerless.

Rooted in the authority of Scripture and fueled by bold, targeted prayers, *Scriptures & Prayers for Combating Spiritual Wickedness* equips you to confront darkness head-on. Each day features a focused Bible passage and a heartfelt, Scripture-based prayer designed to nullify ungodly counsel, disrupt demonic schemes, and establish God's victory in every area of your life.

www.ingramcontent.com/pod-product-compliance
Lightning Source LLC
Chambersburg PA
CBHW060425050426
42449CB00009B/2141